8 Lessons of Self Love

By

Joshalyn K. Stone

© 2021, by Joshalyn K. Stone
All rights reserved, including the right of reproduction in whole or in part of any form.
Printed in the United States of America
ISBN: 978-1-7371235-0-7
Library of Congress Catalog Number: 2021908236

8 Lessons of Self-Love
Written by: Joshalyn K. Stone
Cover Design: German Creative

8 Lessons of Self Love

Table of Contents

Getting to Know Thee J Stone

There comes a time in your life where you just might end up taking advice from someone you've never heard of. You might be able to prevent some of life's hardships through someone else's experiences. As you turn the pages of this book, you'll get to meet different versions of a black queen who has been through tons of obstacles but was strong enough not to break. Some know me as Joshalyn. I grew up with the nickname Puff. My mom calls me Stringfellow (my maiden's name). Yes, I've been married & divorced all before the age of 30. I know that sounds like a lot for some, but that's my reality. Now that we've gotten that out of the way, I also go by Mom to the two little boys who've heard my heartbeat from the inside. That'll always be my favorite name of them all.

Who is Joshalyn? Joshalyn K. Stone is the Founder & Owner of the brand, "I Wasn't Built To Break!!" IWBTW was created in 2018 and legalized in 2020. I created this brand for women by a woman who knows that women tend to bend, but we NEVER

break. In 2018, I decided to put together a seminar for women who

needed to know that they weren't alone in a selfish, cold world. I

wanted them to know that even the happiest person, too, has bad

days. I created this platform because I, too, struggle with many

adversities. The common woman has faced either depression,

anxiety, heartbreak, financial instability, daddy issues, trust issues,

insecurity, body dysmorphia, or literally just being a single mother.

I'm almost 95% sure that every hand that touches this book has

faced at least two of those listed. We all know that the list could

go on. I have now been able to host two successful seminars, and

I'm working on my third. Speaking to women is something I have

always dreamed of doing. I want to teach women that it's ok to

have flaws and fuckups. We have to be strong enough not to

BREAK!

In 2020, I had a thought that became a reality. I decided

to start a live podcast with an unbiased man who would give me

a run for my money. I also knew that the man I chose had to

respect the nature of women. You would think now that we are in

2021, men wouldn't think they were still above us. My brother, Kamau, was the perfect person. Together we decided to call our podcast "All Things Real" because we talk real life, live, with no cut cards. Our first episode debuted on September 10, 2020. We now have 30+ episodes. We get at least 60 live viewers per episode. Once it's posted, we get about 200-800 views per episode.

I was born in 1992, in Baltimore City. I was raised in a household with three brothers and one sister. For most of my non-adult years, my mom was a single mother of five. I watched her struggle at times, even when she had a "man." Sounds bad, right? I took a life lesson from that. No matter how hard life got, you can never give up. If my mother, Kindra Gray, didn't teach me anything, she taught me strength.

I went to elementary school at Johnston Square & Halstead Academy. My middle school days, where I was known as "Joshman" because of my raspy voice, were spent at Loch Raven Academy. My high school years where I learned survival & a voice to gain respect were spent at Kenwood & Overlea. I met my ex-wife at Overlea, and we got married five years later. We spent another 6.5 years married before divorce became our fate. Roch is still one of my closest friends and someone I will always love in this lifetime and the next.

I met "Blac Choc" in the summer of 2009. We dated for three months (90 days exactly) before I gave him some ass. It was funny because I started reading Steve Harvey's book, *Act Like A Lady, Think Like A Man*. Shortly after that I discovered his 90-day rule and went back and counted. I met him on July 31, and our first time was on October 29. It was so weird that it had been exactly ninety days. We were getting busy after that and ended up creating our first love child together. Bralyn is ten now. His father and I didn't work out too much longer after he was born, so we called it quits. I rekindled my relationship with Roch, and we decided to get married two years later. Her and I moved together for the first time when she reported to her second duty station in Fort Campbell, Kentucky. We lived about six miles away in Clarksville, TN. We lived there for about six months before we moved to Oak Grove, Kentucky. I was a full-time student, a first-time stay-at-home mom, and a new military wife all at the same damn time. You can only imagine how my life was going at that time. A few months after I obtained my degree, I moved back to Baltimore so that my first son could experience his first year of school with both of his parents. Probably my biggest regret to this day. I got a job at the Post Office once I got settled back in. I should've gone on to work in the accounting field after working so hard to graduate from college with a 3.9 GPA. Yet 5.5 years later, I'm still at the IMF (Incoming Mail Facility) with my nine lives, as the haters there would say. Especially since I've been escorted out four times because of four different people, three of those times were centered around one damn person I got involved with. Never mix business with pleasure. It's like mixing oil and water. Workplace relations is now a quadruple HELL TO THE NO!! After that relationship crisis, I dated an overseas basketball player for 2.5 years altogether, but not really. Hopefully, you caught my drift. If not, just know we were on and off until my ass got tired of being in a fucked-up situation. Consequently, my situation went from fucked up to real catastrophic quickly.

I met a 20-year-old on Instagram, trying something different. His ass was used to living a fast, carefree life. We hit it off quickly. After years of being told I couldn't bear another child, I ended up pregnant by a kindergartener. That's what my mother refers to him as, lol. I was 27, about to start raising another baby boy, all while trying to help a young man become a father that he wasn't ready to be. I'm 29 now, and I still go through the motions. At times I feel like I don't have a clue where I'm going in life. I really am out here winging it by the day. What I do know, though, is that I refuse to give up.

Dedication

I dedicate this book to every queen across the world who has ever felt alone. To the young girl who feels like she doesn't have a voice. To the young lady whose heart broken and doesn't know how to pick herself up. The girl who looks in the mirror and purposely looks for imperfections because she doesn't feel as pretty as that Instagram model. To the women struggling to take care of a child because the father is too busy living his life. To the mother who's been told that she doesn't deserve a break because she chose to keep her child. To the women who feel like they are never enough. To the working woman who feels like every time she takes two steps forward, she gets knocked ten steps back. To the woman who carries the load of everyone else's baggage and can barely carry her own. To the ladies who feel like they are pushing 30 and still haven't figured life out yet, stop putting someone's else timeline on your clock! I NEED you to stop looking at your glass as half empty but see it as half full. Lastly, I dedicate this book to myself. For always keeping my head above water when it felt like the rest of my body was drowning. As I always say, "I may bend, but I Wasn't Built To Break!!"

I give you my personalized Self Chant for whenever you feel alone. I will also share with you my playlist to get you through tough times.

I, _____, am ME! I am EVERYTHING that I've been through. But I am NOT my past!! I will no longer accept pain or hurt from anyone or anything in my life, including myself. There is nothing or no one in this world that can break me. No matter what I go through, I WILL get through. I will always find my way. I may bend, but "I Wasn't Built To Break!!"

My Top Ten Playlist

1. For Your Glory- Tasha Cobbs

2. I NEED Your Glory- Ernest Pugh

3. Greater Is Coming- Jekalyn Carr

4. The Call- Isabela Davis

5. He Has His Hands On You- Marvin Sapp

6. Let Your Power Fall- FIYA & James Fortune

7. Praise Him In Advance- Marvin Sapp

8. Jacob's Song- Bri Babineaux

9. It Ain't Over- Marietta Brown Clark

10. Raise A Hallelujah- Bri Babineaux

What Is Self-Love?

What is self-love? That's a huge question, right? To many, though, it's just a simple answer, 'I just gotta love myself.' That's a very cliché answer. To others like myself, after the experience, we learn that it's a huge process. It's picking apart your entire self and putting it back together. It's thinking you know at first and realizing you really don't know a got damn thing at all. The ability to acknowledge the good and bad about yourself and really learning to accept your reality is quite a nail-biter. It's going through frustrating moments and dealing with them head-on. We must learn to be completely honest about who we are and what we want to become. If I do say so myself, this isn't a process that happens overnight.

At the age of 29, loving myself is still something that I understand, but I haven't mastered it completely just yet. A lot of my peers think I have it all together because I don't look like what I've been through but by the grace of God. Let me be the first to

12

admit; I am human, just like everyone else around the world. At times, I have bitten off more than I can chew. I have given more than I had to give to suit other people's happiness. I have been heartbroken and depressed trying to raise a newborn baby. I have been betrayed by people I thought loved me. I have hurt other people's feelings by accident. Trust me; I've been through it all. But I'm learning to turn my mistakes into life lessons that I can share with the world.

There are many components to self-love. The most important one is learning to trust yourself. By trusting yourself, you are willing to give yourself credit to make rational decisions that will always benefit YOU! In turn, you'll begin staying true to yourself and choosing only the options that suit you & your happiness first. Always remember, if you don't put yourself first, then who will? Becoming honest with the inner you will force you to be authentic about what you want and expect. You then begin setting standards and boundaries for those who want to grace your presence. If you demand respect, it'll always be given. We don't realize that we teach people how to treat us. I recently was in a complicated situation with my youngest son's father, who's not used to being in a committed, faithful relationship. My brother told me, "As long as you create a stable foundation by setting boundaries and sticking to them, you don't leave any room for disappointment. Every time you *eventually* give in, you are teaching people that you are made of straw. It won't be long before someone comes and blows your house down." That was a mouthful! When I took a step back and picked apart what he was saying, it was true. If your house is leaking water in the kitchen from the bathroom ceiling when it rains, and you keep patching the kitchen ceiling, it will eventually cave in again. You have to start at the root of the problem. Get your ass on top of that roof and seal the damn hole. When we run into problems, we have to learn to tackle them to the best of our ability. If you need help, that's ok too.

I decided to get me a therapist back in 2015. She taught me that if the people around me were scared of my boundaries, those people weren't meant for me. She also taught me that I had to be the person that I wanted others to be to me. You can't expect to receive roses when all you are giving out are thorns. I'm not saying that you'll be perfect. You just need to be ok with making mistakes. After the mistake is made, please do your best to fix it. You wouldn't want someone projecting their self-hate onto you, now, would you?

Learning to Love Yourself First

Love Yourself, they say. Yet, no one tells us how to do such a broad, complex thing. They don't tell us that we have to get real uncomfortable with ourselves and dig deep. They forgot to mention that loving yourself is a lot harder to do. I wasn't taught that it is ok to be selfish at times. Being selfless can cost you your sanity. I know because I've done it over and over and got burned almost every single time.

A few years ago, I was dating a young lady that I had met while working. When I say I thank God, I eventually found the strength to get up, leave, and choose myself; that truly would be an understatement. I had weighed myself down so much with her baggage that I forgot that I, too, needed saving. I stayed in that unhappy situation for almost two whole years. I knew that I deserved better & she knew it too. But I stayed at the time because I didn't know how to put my needs first. Having someone around seemed far easier to deal with rather than not having no one at all. Many of us want love so bad that we sacrifice our morals and

16

values to say we have someone. We get so caught up in trying to prove points to these outsiders when truth be told, it's really out of sight, out of mind. If you are anything like who I used to be, living up to those on social media will definitely run you straight into a dead end.

As mentioned, I was dating a young lady, and I ended up biting off more than I could chew. At the time, I was a single mother, separated from my wife, and I just wanted to have somebody to love. Over the course of two years, I started learning more and more about why I shouldn't have ever dated my love interest at the time. In October of 2016, my late grandmother had come to stay with me. She had been dealing with an overload of seizures and needed help with her everyday life. Due to her experiencing lots of pain, she was prescribed narcotics. After a doctor's visit that didn't go so well, she ended up being transferred to the hospital, where she had a short stay. They then sent her to a rehabilitation center to give her physical therapy. During this time, my ex-girlfriend was staying with me, helping me care for her. This meant she had access to all of her things as much as I did. A few days before Thanksgiving, my mom called me and

asked me to bring over all of my grandmother's meds. Little did I

know, shit was about to go south. I dropped the pills off to her

and went about my day. A few hours later, I received a phone call

that over 20 of my grandmother's OxyContin pills had been

missing. I was so confident that it couldn't be possible because

I've never been a drug user, and I knew I wasn't irresponsible

enough to lose them. I remember the voice I heard on the other

line of the phone. She went on to say, "Ask your girlfriend; she

might have taken them." I said, "Ma, why would she take them?

She doesn't pop pills." She says, "You don't want to believe she

does. Have you not paid attention to her eyes? She always looks

high." I got defensive, and I blurted out, "Ma, why you being like

that? You just want to have a reason not to like her. Ask your

brother. He came over to visit." I just didn't want to believe what

my mom was saying. I hung up and called my girlfriend.

Aggressively I said, "Have you seen my grandmother's pills? My

mom said they are missing." She said, "No. I haven't been in the room since your grandmother left." I hung up, stormed back into my grandmother's room, and researched her closet.

A few hours later, my girlfriend came back into the house, and we started talking about it again. I was going on and on about how much my mom had upset me for accusing her of stealing. She then told me, "I want to tell you something...I took the pills and sold them. I didn't think she would need them, and I needed some extra money." I immediately felt stupid. Like I had been drowning in a pool enclosed with a thick layer of ice. I felt like I had nowhere to run. All I could do was ask why? I felt so many different emotions. I drove to my mom's house, ran in the door, found her, and hugged her with my head on her chest. I started crying because I was so damn embarrassed. My mom tried to explain to me the signs of a person who popped pills. I was disgusted because I never imagined falling in love with someone who did such a thing. I just knew that it was over because how could anyone steal from the elderly? How could you steal from the grandmother of someone you are supposed to love? She and I didn't talk for a few days. I was looking for a reason to forgive her.

I missed her presence and needed her there. So, I thought. I knew that from now on, my trust was broken, and I began showing that.

    I was pushing her away no matter how much she tried to show change. By February 2017, she and I had decided that we would try to take a break. We were trying to work through our problems without being in a committed relationship. I was starting to hold her accountable for her habits. Her drinking was something that ruined us. While I was thinking she was trying to get herself together, little did I know; she started seeing someone else behind my back. Now, I know many people are familiar with the girl who stays just to prove a point. Well, that's who I ended up becoming. The side bitch who was once the only one. I went out of my way to make the new girl feel uncomfortable as much as possible. I even started planning to bring a new life into the world with this woman. She and I decided that in vitro would be our best option, so I started treatment at Shady Grove Fertility. I thank God that I didn't get pregnant. That probably would've been the most selfish decision I ever made.

As time went on, things got worst between us. We both became physical. I had just become a victim and an attacker in such a short period. You would think that would've been enough to walk away for the both of us. On May 20, 2017, things got a lot worst for us than they had ever been. Let's just say she ended up walking out in handcuffs because I had lost my voice due to being chocked. For the first time in my life, I thought that my son would live his life without his mother. I ended up with a $1400 bill from my landlord for damages to the property. Not to mention, some of my furniture had to be replaced. To add insult to injury, I was falsely charged with second-degree assault. Gratefully, I was able to get that expunged off of my record.

My friends knew that I had come to a very low place in my life. I had never put up with that much hurt and disrespect. I also had never been through anything as traumatic in my life. You wouldn't believe that I would have had the courage to walk away even after all of that. In the last six months of that relationship (February to August), I was forcing myself into deeper heartbreak instead of healing. I started becoming angry while trying to find

21

ways to win her back. My mindset was so negative. If I buy her this, she'll come back. If I am her little secret, she will keep me around. I didn't love myself enough to know my worth, which would lead me to walk away with my womanhood. I loved her so much that I forgot about loving me too. I was so blinded by love that I forgot that my peace and sanity were always supposed to come first. I was in a very dark place, and I didn't know where to begin to get myself out. I was struggling on the inside. I was making careless decisions. To the world, though, I was still "Ms. Perfect Patty." When I finally snapped out of it, I realized I was doing all of this just to refrain from sleeping alone. I was doing great at putting on a facade for people who have never even put food on my table.

Sadly, in the world we live in today, a lot of us get caught up in keeping up with society's standards. We don't take the time to actually figure out how to love ourselves properly. We pick apart our lives and try to blame everything and everybody around us for our failures. If I'm extremely honest, we need to start looking in those mirrors that we take 100 selfies in, trying to get the best picture for the most likes and take accountability for who we truly

are.

One day I woke up, and my life had changed. I decided

that having her in my life was not as important to me anymore. At

that moment, I realized that if I couldn't get out of that situation

for me, I had to do it for my son. I started picking myself back up.

I was coming back for my life with a vengeance. I made it clear to

myself that nothing was going to bring me down. By any means

necessary, I was going to get back to embracing who I once was.

I picked up a book by Iyanla Vanzant called, *Yesterday, I Cried*.

That book gave me so much insight into life. It was very relatable

in so many different areas. I started digging deep within myself to

become one with myself. I started taking care of myself physically,

mentally, emotionally, financially. I remembered that I was who I

believed in my heart I was. No one's opinion about me or my

choices in life would no longer define me. I realized that I had to

first love myself in order for someone to love me, so I started

putting the work in. I found myself a big ass broom and started

sweeping around my damn doorstep. I started choosing people

who chose me in front of an audience and not just behind closed doors. I stopped allowing people to make me feel bad about being selfish with my time and attention.

Being alone between relationships was becoming something I knew I needed. I realized that I couldn't change people and how they treated me. Instead, I had to change who was accessible to me. I stopped caring about how society viewed me. If people weren't going to respect me and my boundaries, I had to kick them to the curb. I was finally taking my power back. I am finally ok with people feeling second to me. I learned that no matter what type of relationship it was, whether friend, family member, or spouse, I had to be ok with them not always agreeing with me. Something that really helped with my self-love was writing a positive message on a sticky note every day. I would stick the sticky notes all over my mirror. I started finding peace as the days were going on.

What I took from that heartbreak was that at some point, I had to respect myself enough to let go when it starts to hurt. Who gives a damn anymore what the outsiders have to say? I know now that people can only judge you by what you allow them to have access to. I stopped giving people ammo to shoot at me. I stopped letting the outside world determine how my life was going to be lived. Never short-change yourself. Be ok with making mistakes. Understand that every day you are continuing to grow. What you accept today, you may not accept tomorrow. Love yourself a little harder when times get tough. Never forget that you can't receive love if you don't know how you want to be loved. Keep positive people around you. Don't hang around ten bums because you'll become the eleventh one. To my ladies, if that nigga doesn't change, change niggas!

Seven Dimensions of Well Being

Physically- If you don't like how you look/feel, try eating better or even working out. We use the internet for everything else. Why not look up meal plans that would suit your diet? Drink lots of water to keep yourself from always feeling drained. Take regular trips to see your doctor. Always do your best to get a sufficient amount of rest. Have lots of sex! It's a stress reliever. Just wrap it up.

Emotionally- Stop allowing people to have control over your feelings. It's always ok to cry. Don't make irrational decisions based on temporary feelings. Always tell people how they make you feel before it gets bottled up too much and you explode. Learn the triggers so you can refrain from going from 0 to 100 quickly. Get a therapist to help you dig deep when you can't figure things out on your own. I've had two over the last few years.

Interpersonally- Maintain healthy relationships with those in your everyday life. The ability to have a great support system goes a very long way. Having someone who keeps you on top of your game when you start to fall off in some areas is always a plus. Disconnect from people who always associate you with negativity. Surround yourself with people who add to your growth. If they are not supporting your goals, they are holding you back.

Intellectually- Start looking into things instead of taking people's word for it. Pick up a book or search the internet. Increase your knowledge daily. The bonus is it'll open your mind to brighter ideas that could lead you to something greater. I love talking to people who can keep an intellectual conversation going. Never be afraid to get your questions answered. There's no such thing as a dumb question. But an unasked question can keep you from getting ahead in life.

Spiritually-Create your own relationship with some form of a higher power. To have someone to pray to when things get rough is so therapeutic. Stop telling people everything you have going on. Pray, then meditate. Create a lifestyle habit out of this. Keep at this even when you don't have the best of days. You never know how close you are to your breakthrough. Be still and listen to the universe. Always live by your principles and morals.

Environmentally-Take care of the world around you. The earth takes care of us. Without good air and water, we wouldn't be able to live. Try not to litter and pollute the air. Learn to recycle when possible.

Occupationally- Please choose a job that you love rather than one that pays the bills. If you can have both, great! Being in a toxic work environment is never good. Unnecessary stress isn't good for anyone. Especially when you have to spend a good chunk of your day there, it's ok to use a few vacation days here and there.

I tell my coworker all the time, "Take your time off. This mail will be here when you get back. If you die today or tomorrow, they will just replace you."

When we truly love ourselves, we control our future in every way. We don't wake up looking for ways to make the next person love us. We wake up knowing that we got another shot at being the best version of ourselves. No one's opinion of who we are and what we should be matters anymore. Stop allowing people to jeopardize anything you've worked hard for. We all have shit to lose. Lastly, always remember when you love yourself, you RESPECT YOURSELF!!

Learning That Happiness Is Based On Self

Who in the world makes you the happiest? Cliché question, right? Well, who in the world makes you feel free? If you answered any of those questions without saying, "Me," this is for you. Every now and then, I still have to remind myself that I'm in total control of my happiness. Now I'm not saying that people or things can't add to our happiness because my two boys bring me joy like no other. I am saying that every day I wake up, I choose whether or not I'll be happy. A lot of us don't realize that we choose sadness. We choose to let small situations become bigger than they have to be. We dwell on our past traumas/behaviors instead of accepting things for what they are and moving forward.

I used to let things I knew inevitably I couldn't change bother me. We forget that we have the choice to decide how we let things affect our daily life. I know that ignoring those things mentioned above is easier said than done because we are human, and things upset us.

Being happy with yourself means a number of things. The main thing is being comfortable doing things alone. Sometimes being alone can be the most peaceful thing a person can do. I remember after I graduated from high school, I went back to visit my favorite teacher. We were having a very good conversation when she asked me what I had planned to do over the next few months with my time. I had been a mother for a few years now, so it was only right that my response was, "I want to travel." She then asked me, "What's stopping you?" I responded, "I don't want to get on a plane and spend time in an unfamiliar city with people I don't know. Plus, I never have anyone to go with." I did not know that she would give me a speech that would stay with me forever. She came back and said, "Young lady, do you not know how much time you are wasting. You'll be waiting a lifetime for people to do things with you. You have to learn to do things on your own." She went on and on about how she would go to bars alone and meet new people. She would even travel out of state on business and network with people who would eventually become lifelong friends. Here I am, a woman in her prime, and I couldn't even take a trip to the mall alone. She had given me a serious reality check.

Everything she was saying was starting to make sense all of a sudden. I began thinking back to when I would ask a friend to join me on a trip and how many different excuses they would come up with. And if it wasn't an excuse to them, it seemed as though it was to me. "Girl, I gotta pay this bill. I know I'll have the money for the flight, but I might not be able to put up for the hotel. I don't have a babysitter." It was always something. Then I thought about all the times I did go on vacation with people and was so damn miserable. I went to Puerto Rico once, and one of the girls who came, that I didn't know, ended up with my Pandora bracelet. I was uncomfortable the rest of the trip because I didn't know her enough to know if she was a thief or was actually going to give me my bracelet back without me looking around for it.

A few weeks after she and I had the conversation, I built my courage up to head on into Fridays to sit at the bar and write. When I first got there, I was super nervous. I kept looking around, thinking someone was going to be looking at me. I ordered my first drink and my famous order of buffalo wings. I pulled my book

31

out and began to write. After the first twenty minutes, all the uneasiness went down the drain. I felt alive in my presence. I knew that this could become something that I could do every now and then. Writing and having my favorite drink (Amaretto Sour) at the bar is now something that I can truly enjoy. I had stopped being insecure about being by myself. I actually didn't realize how much peace I would find in doing simple things alone, especially because I'm still working on having patience with people when it comes to my time.

In February 2018, I decided to visit my ex-girlfriend in France. I had to get on a foreign plane and fly seven hours across the Atlantic Ocean. That was the scariest plane ride I have ever taken in my life. The entire ride, I kept thinking, "Act as if you belong here so you won't get taken." On that flight, I was learning a lot about myself. If I could go to a foreign country where I couldn't speak their language, it wasn't anywhere in the world I couldn't travel alone anymore. I ended up traveling back to France at the end of that year. By the beginning of 2019, I started moving so freely. I genuinely became comfortable in my skin. I was ok with making decisions on my own, no matter how anyone else would feel about it. Everything I once was afraid to do, I started checking off. Staying true to myself was keeping me happier than I had ever been. The type of peace I had found felt good. It was so good that it spilled over into other areas of my life. Things I used to let get to me didn't anymore. I stopped needing other people's validations for things I enjoyed doing. If you claimed to be my friend and chose not to support me, your loss, not mine. I learned that giving people a chance to explain the unanswered why's was only giving them room to make excuses.

As I previously mentioned, excuses tend to get under my skin. In turn, it interrupts my peace. I struggled for a long time with validating my "friends" excuses just because I felt like I needed them around to make me happy. Looking back, it was the things we did together and how we interacted that boosted my happiness. I remember always trying to explain why certain things happened or even correcting people's thoughts about me. It was important that I cleared up rumors because I didn't want to be judged by lies. Ask me today to clear up anything, and the shit is just not happening. What I've learned is that we can't change people's opinions of us. It's just that—their opinion. You and I won't ever be able to control how people view us. I stopped giving my energy to situations that were out of my hands.

While learning how to keep myself happy, I started researching how to deal with stress. Stress can ruin your sense of peace if you allow it to. Most of us nowadays run to the bar or the weed man every time we run into a problem. In reality, all that does is slow down the process of getting to the root of the problem and reaching a solution. The quicker we deal with the problematic things around, the easier it'll be to remain calm.

Over the last two months, I've been facing plenty of things that have put me on edge. Imagine finding ways to have extra income because you want to buy a house. Whether working late, doing hair on the side, or selling items you can profit from. In about three weeks, you've managed to save close to $2000 extra. Next thing you know, you take a trip to the dentist. He tells you that he's going to give you a fill-in because your wisdom tooth has grown crooked and has caused a small cavity in an area that you couldn't clean. He then suggests that you go to an endodontic specialists to make sure you don't need a root canal. You schedule the appointment and have the consultation. They proceed to tell you that you'll have a copay of a little over $300. You think, ugh, I don't want to spend this money, but I know I want my teeth to be in the best condition possible. After getting the procedure done, the endodontist instructs you to return to the dentist to get the final fill and cap. This meant I had to take off from work which means no overtime for that day. On the day of my dentist appointment, I walked up to the desk to sign in. The secretary greets me and says, "Hey, Ms. Stone. Did anyone speak to you about your copay today? Your balance is $972." I immediately got frustrated. In my mind, all I could think about was the fact that I didn't take off to lose out on money and still turn around and kick out close to $1,000. I really couldn't believe what I was hearing. I sat down and thought about leaving. But then, after thinking about how much time I would've wasted missing work and having to take off still to get it done eventually, I decided to say screw it. I might as well get it done now. I sat through that procedure for almost an hour, so upset. All I could think about was how I couldn't get ahead. I talked about it for almost a week before I just accepted the situation for what it was. The money was already spent.

As the days went on, I tried to figure out ways not to miss work and make extra money. We got hit with snow the following day, and because I have a Jeep, I decided I could still go to work. On my way there, I had the heat blasting because my windows were fogged. Before I knew it, the crack in my windshield spread faster than you could count to three. I immediately wanted to just sulk in my sadness. Why was everything continuing to go wrong all of a sudden? Driving with my ten-month-old and ten-year-old while my windshield was damaged was not something I could see myself doing for more than a day. I called my insurance company and filed a claim. Well, there goes another $250 for my deductible I had to kick out. You can only imagine how stressful things were becoming for me. I started to feel like I couldn't win for losing. A special man in my life reminded me that I needed to remain optimistic and find a way to see the positive side of things. The fact that I could afford to handle my business right away was enough for me to be grateful. I wasn't looking at it like that from the beginning, though. I was letting things I couldn't control, control my emotions and stress me out. After praying about my situation, I let it go and left it up to God. Trying to remain stress-free, at peace, and happy is definitely a huge task. It's something that every person has to fight to do. It's very easy to get discouraged about things going on in your life and feel like you're failing. I know because I have those struggles too. We all have to wake up every single day and CHOOSE. Choose to be happy. Choose to let go of self-limiting behaviors. Choose to let go of stressors. Choose to smile. Choose to make someone else smile. Choose to protect your peace. Choose to spend time with yourself. Choose to have the right people around us. Choose to focus on changing the things you can and not things you can't. Choose to focus on what you have and not what you don't. Choose to be honest. Simply just start choosing because you have the choice to decide. Happiness is a choice. Peace is a choice. Never forget that.

I have now decided that I will always do my best to choose happiness. Do I expect things always to be perfect? Absolutely not! But I found ways to cope with stress because the happier I am, the happier my kids will be. When I'm having a frustrating day, I pull out my book and write. I even turn on one of my favorite playlists and let the music soothe my mind. If it's a nice day, I can take a walk. If I can get through the rough days, so can you. 😊.

Learning the Things We Dislike About Ourselves

Have you ever taken the time to ask yourself the different things you honestly dislike about yourself? If you have, do you have reasons as to why? Are these dislikes things that can be fixed? If so, what will you do to start the process of changing those things? I strongly encourage you to figure these things out. I believe that this is a very important part of growth. You become better for yourself and the people around you. There are a lot of things that I dislike about my personality. The main things are being a good-hearted person to people who don't deserve it and being very prideful.

I've always been willing to give those around me the shirt off my back. At times, I would even take food off my plate to make sure my friends were good. Although I strongly believe doing things from the heart will only in return fill your life with blessings. But, at times, this has been one of my biggest downfalls. I think

I'm doing something to better others, and it ended up biting me in my ass.

About five years ago, I met this girl while hanging out with one of my closest friends. We saw each other over the course of the next three years anytime our mutual friend would host an event. In 2018, I moved to Harford County, maybe about half a mile from where the girl resided. Over the next few years, she and I formed a friendship. During the summer of 2019, we had gotten close. Especially since I felt like she was a genuine person with a good heart. At the end of that summer, I had gotten pregnant by a young man who wasn't quite ready to take on the role of being a father. Therefore, I was subjected to doing my pregnancy alone. My close friends, she included, became my moral support system.

During my pregnancy, I became a high risk for myself and the baby. I became very stressed and emotional for the last five months of my pregnancy. She was more accessible to me than any of my other friends because she lived the closest. Naturally, I began confiding in her about my life. All the things I had been through and was still going through. I even trusted her with the spare key to my house. Eventually, she was starting to share with me the problems she was experiencing with her credit. "Ms. I always have to cross the ocean for people who wouldn't even cross the street for me" decided to offer a helping hand. I added her to my credit card as an authorized user. Although I kept the card in my possession, it still would help her credit boost because I managed my credit very well. I will never take full credit for anything that someone else has accomplished. But let's call an ace an ace and a spade a spade. Within the next few months, she was able to make a big purchase sooner than she would've been if she did it on her own.

After I had my youngest son in April 2020, his dad and I decided to give our family a shot. I knew in my mind that it would come with a lot because of the age difference in itself. As my friend, I thought I could share many of the things that he and I were going through in confidence. She had known more about me than any other person I spoke with during that time. In October of 2020, she and I were having a phone conversation about our mutual friend. During the conversation, she and I disagreed about one of the statements she had made about our mutual friend. Within the next few weeks, I had gotten a phone call from our friend, and boy did she flip the script. I was told so many hurtful things that she had said about me. She had said that she only got close to me during my pregnancy because she had felt sorry for me. She was tired of hearing about my relationship problems because I chose to deal with someone, she tried to warn me about. She continued to say she would not watch my podcast because all I did was tell the world too much of my business.

I use my experiences to encourage people to be authentic with themselves about things we all struggle with in reality. The thing that hurt the most was the lie she had told. She told our mutual friend that she was going to ask to be removed from my credit card because I was making her credit score drop. I was so upset about that. I couldn't believe those words had been coming out of the other side of the phone. Now, anyone who knows me knows if I don't do anything right, I pay my bills on time. I was so ticked off that I logged into my credit card portal and screenshotted my history to our friend. I haven't missed an on-time payment since I opened the account in March of 2018. How could someone I did so much for, use, and abuse my love for them like that?

   I never count favors because I genuinely do them. I called my three good girlfriends on three-way and told them what had just happened. My son's godmother was the most appalled. She started reminding me of how during my pregnancy, I would get out of my bed on Friday and Sunday nights to pick the girl up from her weekend job. She was missing out on a lot of money because her business took a serious hit during COVID, so I collected funds from my friends on her behalf. How I would find things around my house for her to clean just to give her an extra few dollars even though I wasn't working myself. I had been out of work from March to October because I had a new baby, and Covid was at an all-time high. I started remembering how much of myself I was putting on the line to keep her head above water. Sissy Pooh E, gave me a serious earful. "Don't you ever do no shit like that again? I don't care who it is. It's one thing to help your friends Puff. But, you do too much. You go above and beyond all the time, and people use you." I still remember those words screeching at my ears. It was going to be a cold day in hell before I ever let someone use my good heart against me again.

A few days later, I got a call from our mutual friend, and she said to me, "I'm sorry she did that to you, Puff. I wanted to tell you what type of person she is. I just didn't want you to think I was hating on ya'll friendship because ya'll got close when you and I weren't speaking." From that moment, it made me feel like I could never trust a new person because you never know what their true intentions are. People see me and see my heart. Some appreciate me for being genuine. Others, well, they don't have a good heart, so they see me as a way to come up. Being a giver only allows people to take, take, take. My biggest downfall was thinking, "Nah...they wouldn't do me like that." Yet, they would do me just like that. What makes me different from that person's mother or sister whose names she would drag through the mud? Getting comfortable with not being "Miss Nice Girl" was a task I had to start working on. Trying to differentiate between who's really for you and against you is so hard. Sadly, from now on, if I can't ask for it in return, I am no longer willing to give it out.

Pride will kill you. That was the saying I had always heard growing up. But for me, it was something that as I got older, I started suffering from more. Asking people for anything, whether an item or just help, became tremendously hard for me. Expressing myself about my feelings was something I couldn't stand. Me being vulnerable was just a simple Hell No! In 2014, I had gotten married to the person that I knew I loved. Although things weren't perfect between us, we still felt like marriage would benefit both of us. I moved out of state, ready for a change, to be with her while she served the country. I picked up my life and moved twelve hours away from my family to Tennessee to build a life of my own.

During the first year there, I became solely dependent on her while I finished college to obtain my degree. You can only imagine how many times what was being done for me was thrown in my face. I had to hear no at times when I wanted certain things. When I expressed my concerns about certain things, it went in one ear and out the other. Expressing my feelings was a waste of time.

When my feelings got hurt, I just kept it to myself. I learned to deal with it on my own. Over time, her throwing things in my face had gotten better, but I had already begun building up a wall. I became very uncomfortable with revealing my true feelings. Anytime someone would offer to do things for me, I would immediately decline because I was afraid it would be later used against me.

In December of 2020, my brother and I had an episode on our podcast about pride. He said, "When people say that they're prideful and stuff like that, in my mind, in my weird little mind, that translates as them saying, 'Hey, I'm scared.'" I had never looked at it in that sense. I didn't realize I was afraid of being vulnerable. That episode had come at the perfect time because I had been dealing with this guy I met in July, and he was someone who deserved more of me than what I had been giving. On his 28th birthday, some female in his life had posted a pic of him with a lengthy caption about how much she cared about him. Of course, he reposted it. It wasn't the picture that had bothered me. When I read the words, I Love You; my eyes had seen a ghost. I left clicked the story on his Instagram to go back and reread it. I instantly felt a way and started pulling back expeditiously.

Over the next month, the distance was all he could feel between us. I was such a bitch at times for absolutely no reason at all. He kept asking me what changed. I refused to tell him how I felt because I didn't want him to know that I cared about him. I was afraid to ask a simple question. I didn't want him to give me an answer that my heart wasn't ready to hear. How could I honestly feel some type away about anything when he and I had yet to discuss being exclusive? I kept my mouth shut and my feelings hidden. I ended up allowing myself to go back to my previous relationship, where I knew I would only experience more hurt. I had a bad concept that I lived by, stick with who you know because you already know what you are dealing with. Yeah, that led me down a road to destruction. I could've prevented all of the unnecessary drama that came a month later. I ended up almost losing a man who all-around was genuinely a great guy.

When I finally took my brother's advice. I asked him about the female a few weeks later. The girl ended up being a long-time friend who had been there for him when he experienced all that life was throwing at him. I felt so damn dumb. I could've alleviated thirty-plus days of BS by simply asking a question. I had learned a lesson of a lifetime. These days, I am overly speaking my mind, lol. If something is bothering me, I will take time to calm my nerves and bring it up once I'm level-headed. Having pride issues is something a lot of people face. We don't take into consideration how it could affect others. It leads you to down a path where you don't take chances—not realizing that those chances could change your life in a great way. Being less prideful has kept me from overthinking situations that would replay over and over again in my mind until I got an answer. Working on my pride has been one of the best things I've done. It is still a work in progress, but I'm a lot further than I was three months ago.

Learning To Embrace Our Flaws

Hey Siri, play "Naked" by Ella Mai. I remember when I was In France, and I heard this song for the first time. I believe that was the first time I heard a whole song that spoke about flaws that I could relate to. Just like the average person, I struggle to accept my imperfections.

When I was a preteen, I started developing acne. I hated it so much because my classmates could tell exactly when I was going through puberty. Those damn menstrual bumps would always appear in the middle of my damn cheek. I tried so many things over the years. I used to scrub my face so hard with soap trying to make the marks disappear. For some reason, I was born with oily skin, so it's easy for my pores to get clogged. Proactiv had become very popular, so of course, I had begged my mom to buy it for me. That didn't work. Eventually, my only other choice was to go to a dermatologist. I finally thought I had the cure. He prescribed me clindamycin to use twice a day. After thirty days of using it, I still showed no results. Nothing seemed to work. I began getting fake hair installed to cover the sides of my face. My natural hair was a good length, but it just wasn't thick enough. You could see straight through it. Another epic fail. That made my breakouts even worst.

As I got older, I came to the conclusion that what I ate and drank had a lot to do with my breakouts. A few years ago, I had done a ten-day detox because I was trying to lose weight. The detox consisted of nothing but fresh fruit and veggies. No sugar, no starch, no salt, no dairy. Much of nothing. I drank lots of water too. I thought I was only doing my stomach justice, but I started seeing a change in my face as well. I had finally found the cure. My skin had started to glow so much that I was getting compliments left and right. Water had become my best friend. I immediately turned that ten-day detox into a lifestyle change. I became a pescatarian. I was beyond grateful because not only did my body look better, my face had taken a turn for the better.

Joshman is the name my middle school classmates had given me. I had the deepest voice in the school, and everyone made fun of me because of it. I hated how I sounded and would try to use alternative voices when speaking in front of the class. I never really wanted to participate, but I did because I was one of the smartest kids in the class. To make matters worse, I loved R&B music, so I would randomly burst out into a chorus at times. This didn't go so well. Especially when I was home, my entire household would yell across the house, "Shut up, Puff!" I will never forget I was in the bathroom singing one day. Avant had come out with a new single, and it was a hit. The song was blasting through my speakers as I sang along, "I know you wanna rub. I know you wanna touch. I know you wanna feel. So baby, keep it real." My brother came out of his room and said, "That's a nice song. Who sings it?" I responded, "Avant." Before I could get back to my jam, he laughed and said, "Well, let him sing it then." I felt so dumb as I stood there—humiliation at its finest. I hated my voice even more after that day. How could God give me a voice like this that I'd be stuck with for the rest of my life?

The summer before I went to high school, I knew that I would switch up the narrative. If I didn't make it so obvious that my voice bothered me, people wouldn't use it against me. It was

51

time that I accepted my voice for what it was. Even though I knew I couldn't sing, I sang loud and proud around my house. When I got to high school that year, I went with more confidence. Those little evil middle school classmates were gone. I had a chance at a fresh start. I made it up in my mind that my voice didn't make me. My personality did. What helped even more, was that I became a little more attractive. The teenage boys and girls made that known without question. How I sounded wasn't at the forefront of my mind anymore. It wasn't talked about it on an everyday basis anymore unless I was too loud in class. My teachers would kindly pull me to the side and remind me that I was much louder than the rest of the class because my voice carries. I appreciated them for that because they weren't trying to embarrass me. I finally believed in my heart that the coast was clear after I had graduated from high school. Welp, that wasn't until my ex-girlfriend and I relationship had ended for good in 2009.

During our last argument, she mortified me. She told me that she hated having sex with me because of how I sounded when I moaned. To make matters worse, she sounded it out. I was crushed at the moment, and all my middle school trauma rushed back to the forefront of my brain. She was a mean little bitch at that moment. The funny thing is, twelve years later, we still see each other. And every time, she still asks can she hit it one more time. I'm 29 now, and sometimes I still forget how unique and distinct my voice is from everyone else's around me. But I've accepted how I sound. I can care less about who wants to hear me and who doesn't. I even have concerts on Instagram at least once a month. The world is going to hear my voice, and my mother is going to continue to tell me, "Don't quit your day job."

It's not how you look on the outside, but what you put out from the inside. Yeah, that sounds good. Whoever came up with that phrase was lying. And if they weren't, society sure has a funny way of encouraging people to embrace their natural-born bodies. After having my son in 2011, I never really took the time to lose weight. In 2017, I decided that all of that baby fat had to get gone. I always had thick legs, and some love handles, but I couldn't stand the muffin top. I became a critic about how I looked to myself in the mirror. At the time, I was roughly 183 pounds. I had just come back from Puerto Rico two months prior on an all-girls trip. I started looking back at the pics of us on the beach. Boy, did I have some nerve to be wearing a two-piece with all my gut hanging out the sides of my bottom. I was disgusted. I couldn't believe I had the courage to wear something like that out in public. I started comparing my pics with other people's pictures on social media. I started asking around to find ways to help me lose weight. My coworker suggested that I see a physical trainer who hosted a boot camp in Timonium, MD. I was serious about it, so I called him immediately.

Per our conversation, we agreed that I should start the following Monday and begin my 30-day training. I was so eager to lose weight that having asthma wasn't even considered. During workouts, I would feel my chest tightening while the taste of blood filled my mouth. If this ever happened to you, then you know what's possibly to come. I could've had an asthma attack that would land me right in the hospital. That wasn't enough for me to quit. After my first thirty days, I saw results, just not the ones I was looking for. I had a weight goal of 165 pounds. Therefore, I joined again. I did this from November of 2017 to February 2018. I decided to also tack on a ten-day smoothie cleanse while I was in the program. I immediately started seeing results and became extremely happy. I ordered a ton of new crop tops to show off my slim & trim new figure that I had worked hard for. Posting full body pics on Instagram for validation was just what I did. I felt good, but after a few months, I still was not satisfied. I turned the ten-day cleanse into a lifestyle to keep the results I already had. A few months later, I had helped a coworker out and let her become my roommate. I told her about my weight loss issues that I struggled with for almost a year and a half. I lost the weight, but I still didn't look the way social media said I should look. She replied, "Girl, you crazy. You suffer from body dysmorphia." "Body what," I thought to myself. I immediately picked up my phone to google it. The webpage read exactly what I was feeling. It described me to a T.

I spent hours a day trying to figure out how I could get the body I wanted without going under the knife. Although I had gotten down to 158lbs and was able to wear waist beads & two pieces, I still wasn't pleased. Just my luck, after working out and changing my eating habits, I ended up pregnant at the end of the summer. Gosh, darn it. I had a plan to control my eating habits so that I wouldn't gain too much weight. From September to December, I hadn't gained 1 pound. My doctor started getting concerned. She told me that if I didn't gain at least five pounds within the next three weeks, she would send me to a gastroenterologist. At that point, I could be affecting the baby. I never felt so vile in my life. For the next few weeks, I ate every time I had the urge to. My selfish ways weren't worth me harming my baby. I went through the rest of my pregnancy as I should have. I was a whopping 197 pounds when I gave birth to a handsome and healthy baby boy on April 13, 2020. I was blessed, but I couldn't help but think about how I wasted the last 2-3 years working for a body all to gain at least 30lbs back.

Since I had a cesarean section, I had developed more scar tissue as if I didn't have enough from my first born. Since I breastfeed, I couldn't go back to detoxing right away. In December of 2020, I talked to my friends and my therapist about getting liposuction done. They encouraged me and told me I looked perfectly fine for a woman who had given birth less than a year ago. I also returned to work that month and received a ton of compliments. I appreciated it a lot because I was always discouraged about my weight. I stopped stepping on the scale every day, looking for a lower number to pop up. I became a lot more comfortable with my body after the encouragement I received.

With social media being a big thing, it's hard to accept your appearance without wanting to make a change. But remember, God says that we are wonderfully made. No matter how we may see ourselves in the mirror, God sees our hearts. After years of struggling with my flaws, I finally embraced them. Somethings we aren't able to change about ourselves. How we look will never supersede how we treat others. I look and sound different from anyone else on the planet. That's what makes me unique.

Learning to Take Advice
But Making Our Own Decisions

Friend Diaries 101.....Every time I turn around, a new situation is on the rise. At the moment, we pick up that phone and call whoever is closest to us. Me, well, I send out a mass text individually to all my friends. Now, how smart is that when a ton of opinions fill my head? A clouded judgment is never good when your life is about to change forever.

8/27 20:31 Toxic: Yo get the abortion 💯
8/27 20:31 Me: That's not who I am.
8/27 20:31 Toxic: Yo get the abortion 💯 I will hate you forever on some shit like that.
8/27 20:32 💯 This what you trynna do is not kool.
8/27 20:32 Me: What am I trying to do? Like what?
8/27 20:32 Toxic: Trying to fuking keep it.
8/27 20:33 Me: SMDH
8/27 20:33 Toxic: Get rid of it
8/27 20:34 💯 💯
8/27 20:48 Me: I asked you to simply give me some time to think about things. I asked you to wait til my appt. you couldn't even do that. You're fucking selfish. And if you going hate me for not doing what you want me to do without considering my feelings, then that's fine. I don't need your smart ass antics right now. So miss me with the bullshit. When you ready to be an adult about the situation, then we can talk. Until then, I'm done going back and forth!
8/27 21:07 Toxic: Get rid of it 💯 💯 💯 end of conversation.

I couldn't bear another minute talking about this, so I stopped responding. At the age of 27, I had gotten pregnant by a 20-year-old who just wasn't ready. I called my girls up and just cried. I was about to make the worst decision of my life. When I got myself together, I remembered taking my god sister to get an abortion back in 2012. Although I didn't go through it, watching her force a miscarriage scarred me for life. I didn't want to be the girl driving home from the clinic and bleeding through my clothes because I couldn't make it home. My passenger seat had been stained from a blood clot that she had passed on our drive home. I snapped back to reality quickly and decided that I needed some advice from people who experienced it. I called three of my friends individually and asked a series of questions. Why did you get one? Do you regret it? How far along were you when you got it? How did it affect your body? They all answered differently. One even mentioned that she did it because having a baby by someone who didn't want the child would cause too much conflict. The way society goes, once he says he wouldn't be there, 99.9% of the time, he wouldn't. That response pierced my chest.

I knew it would be hard to go through a pregnancy alone, but I hoped that he would eventually come around. I made the last phone call to an associate who had just gone through it about a month before. She told me that her abortion went wrong and led her back to the surgery room to get a D&C. They had left small parts of the fetus inside of her. I couldn't imagine going through with an abortion, trying to process it mentally, to find out later that it was done incorrectly. I had a whole lot to think about. I called my three bonus sisters up, and of course, for them, it was a HELL TO THE NO! They were against it for many reasons. The main reason was they had known how long I had prayed for this moment.

Back in 2017, I was diagnosed with menorrhagia. The odds of me being able to get pregnant again were slim to none. Before I could make a final decision, I had to talk to my mom about it. We were standing in her kitchen almost three weeks later of finding out. I blurted it out. "Ma, I'm pregnant." She replied, "Mmhm, you done got pregnant by a kindergartner. You just kept sneaking off to Ellicott City. Welp, that's going to be grand baby number twelve. She's going to be a chocolate drop just like her daddy with my eyes." She knew that I wasn't going to get an abortion before I could even mention it. I became very emotional at that moment. She had just spoken exactly what I dreamed of my daughter to be. I knew that I had to make my mind up after that. I went home that night and weighed my options. I even called him to see if he had a change of heart. He didn't, of course. Instead, he told me all the reasons why he wasn't ready. He was too young. He was just getting the recognition for his barbering career that he had worked so hard for. We barely knew each other. He wanted to have his own barbershop before he had any children. He had just graduated high school a few months ago, so he was still trying to figure life out. I started taking the things he was saying into consideration. For the first time in my life, I was willing to neglect my morals to please him knowing I wouldn't be able to live with such regret. He had convinced me to make the appointment.

I called around the following week and had finally landed an appointment. On September 16, 2019, I was going to get rid of my unborn child. As the days were counting down, I got more and more anxious. It was Sunday, Sept 8, and I had a big ass meltdown. I knew that, deep down, this was not something I wanted to do. I picked up my phone to dial a friend. Ring. Ring. Ring......you have reached the voicemail box of.... No answer. I was losing it. Then it dawned on me that I forgot to call on the one person who could help me see clearly. It was time for me to get on my knees and pray. I went to bed that night, waiting for the morning. I knew that I would wake up with a clear mind and a sound heart. Instead, I woke up the next morning frantic. I couldn't take the anticipation anymore. It was either I was going to get it in the next day or two, or I wasn't going to get it at all. It was killing me just imagining it.

I called up my good sister Erica, who was also pregnant at the time and just had a moment of truth. I knew in my heart that I would regret every moment I lived if I had gone through with it. She supported my decision and told me that I owed it to Mr. Toxic to tell him right away. It was time to face reality. I texted him.

9/7 13:56 Me: I can't handle all of this anymore. I have to really focus on myself. I have to really get back to me and my own happiness. I really wanted to continue to get to know you, but it's not worth me feeling the way I've been feeling. I hope you

continue to grow in your business and become as successful as you plan. I just gotta let this small chapter of my life go. 😞
9/7 13:58 Toxic: Damn, that's krazy 🗿
9/7 14:07 Me: I'm not sure when you'll have time to get my things together, but you can either send them to my house, or we can meet.

I had made my decision to keep my baby whether I had the father's support or not. I had moments where I felt bad. I never wanted to be the person who made someone else feel like their feelings didn't matter in a situation like this. But to me, my sanity was way more important. How could I continue to raise my oldest son if I was depressed for years to come? I couldn't imagine being the girl who lived with regret wondering about those what-ifs. That was a decision that, once made; you could never turn back. I went through my pregnancy alone. I was scared. I was afraid. I was lonely. I hated the fact that I had to experience my first gender reveal alone. But I knew that I was going to be blessed at the end of my pregnancy. When I reached 7.5 months, he and I began communicating more often. There were more arguments than anything, though. To my surprise, he offered to attend my baby shower. Due to Covid-19, I just had a drive-by shower, and he came over to assemble all of the baby's furniture. He also decided

that it was important that he was present for the birth of his first

child. His only wish was granted when I named our son after him.

Things haven't always been sweet, but I must say he's come a long

way during our son's first year of life.

    Deciding to keep my son was one of the hardest decisions

I had to make. It was also one of the hardest things I've ever had

to experience. But with God, I am getting through. Just because

someone has dealt with the same thing you're going through

doesn't mean your outcome will follow suit. Always follow your

heart and make decisions that you can live with. Only you get to

walk in your shoes.

Learning to Stop Unsatisfying Self To Satisfy Someone Else

In the matter of United States vs. Joshalyn Stone, your motion for Chapter 7 bankruptcy has been granted. At the age of 22, I had fallen into debt because saying no wasn't something I felt was easy to do.

Growing up in the house with my mother, taking care of business was instilled in us. I knew that by any means necessary, bills came first, playtime was last. After having my first son at eighteen, I knew it was a must that I was financially responsible. His dad and I lived in his mother's house, so I was able to save enough money whenever we decided to move out. Unfortunately, he and I went our separate ways, so I moved into my own place when Bralyn was almost two years old. I promised myself that I would never pay rent or my car payment late, no matter how hard times would get. My son needed a place to live, and we needed a way to get around. I knew in my heart that I never wanted a reason to move back home.

By the time I was 21, I was able to get credit lines that most people my age could only dream of. My bank at the time offered me a $7,000 credit limit that I honestly knew I didn't need. I couldn't believe it, so of course, I wanted to brag about it. One of my family members then came to me with her problems. She said that she was behind on her rent and needed some food in her house, so she asked to borrow $2,000. I didn't think it was a good idea, but I honestly felt bad for her situation. As bad as I wanted to say no, I couldn't because this was someone who had practically raised me. She told me that she would give me the money back over the next month's span once she got her settlement check. I took her word for it and marched right up to the bank and made a cash advance for the entire $2,000. They informed me that I wouldn't accrue interest as long as I paid it back within ninety days. That was more than enough time for her to give me the money back.

Four months had passed, and she still hadn't given me a dollar back. I didn't want to seem like a pest, but the interest had started to accrue at 13%. I decided to finally reach out, but it was always an excuse. I decided that I would give her some more time because I understood that life just happens sometimes unexpectedly. Meanwhile, I was preoccupied with being a newlywed and enjoying my new home in Tennessee anyway. It became routine for me to travel back to Baltimore at least once or twice every other month to bring Bralyn back and forth to see his dad. I always had to visit my friends. One friend, in particular, was living at home with her mother, so I'd see her mom often too.

During one of my stays, her mom had asked if I could add her to my cell phone plan. I told her that I shared an account on my wife's line and wouldn't do that without her permission. She then went as far as asking if I could just get her a line with another carrier. Here I am thinking about the debt I'm already in with a bank. I just didn't want to do it. Me being young and naïve, I did it anyway. I went back home with a feeling that it just wouldn't go right. A few months had passed before I took another visit to Baltimore to celebrate with my sister and my friend Dezire's birthdays. I decided that I would stay with my friend and her mom, especially since she would attend the DC party with me. Because I had flown into town, I didn't have my car. I called my mom to ask her if I could use her car for the night. My friend's mom had overheard my conversation and offered to let me use her car. I was skeptical because I never been a fan of using anyone else's car unless I was on their insurance. I don't like the feeling of being responsible for property that isn't mine. After about an hour, she had finally convinced me. We went to the party and the night was young. I didn't do much of any drinking for two reasons. One, I didn't care for most of Dezire's friends and always wanted to be alert. Two, I knew I had someone else's car and didn't want to risk getting pulled over in D.C.

We returned to my friend's house that night without having any issues. A few days later, I flew back home to Tennessee. I got a text from my friend saying that her mother said we damaged her car and wanted me to pay $700 cash for it. I told her that I couldn't have done that because we were together the entire time. Her mother still insisted that I was responsible. She knew that my wife was in the military, and she assumed that we were flooded in cash. I told her mother that I wasn't working, so I couldn't afford that type of money and why couldn't she go through her insurance. She told me that I should ask my wife. I let her know that my wife would not be held responsible for anything she had nothing to do with. I also mentioned that I would help out as much as I could when I could. It wasn't a rush for me because I knew certainly that I didn't do such a thing. About two weeks later, I received an email stating that another two lines were added to my cell phone plan. I didn't mention it to her because I thought she would do the right thing. I decided that after a month went by to check on the bill and what did I see. A turn-off notice with a past due balance of almost $1,100 with a total amount due of $1,452 and some change. It was excruciating to see. All I could think about was the fact that at the age of 22, I had let two people bamboozle me into debt that, ultimately, I would be responsible for. I refused to pay those bills, though, because I didn't think it was fair. You better bet the bill collectors could care less when they sent those bills right into collections. I decided to say fuck everything and file bankruptcy. It was no way in hell that I was going to pay almost 4K in bills for services I didn't use. At the time, I knew nothing about consolidation loans or settlements. If I did, I would've gone that route. I had made a decision that would stick with me for the next seven years.

From the moment my case was settled, I told myself that I would never put anything in my name for anyone unless I had sole control of how it was being used. I was through with saying yes when deep down, I wanted to say no. The majority of the time, I was trying to prove my loyalty to people who took advantage of me. There were times where I would burn a hole in my pocket to see someone else not take a fall. I didn't understand that if a person couldn't afford it on their own, they didn't need it. I was putting people's wants and needs before my own. I even remember one time I only had enough gas to get me to and from work. A friend called me and asked for a ride, and I called my wife to give me gas money. The older I got, the more I realized that it's ok to say NO. Suppose I'm not comfortable with a certain situation going on that I needed to express it. People will feel a certain way, but eventually, they will get over it. The ones who are genuinely for you will understand that you are entitled to saying no. They won't even part their lips even to ask you to do certain shit. This goes for our relationships as well. These days I do a lot better standing firm on what I believe in. I am not saying that it's not ok to compromise at times. Just compromise for those willing to reciprocate. As long as it's not a drastic decision, I am always open to the discussion.

Learning To Forgive
When There Is No Apology

"You know if that man press charges on your brother, you could go to jail too, right?" Fifteen years later and those words have never left my brain. Those words still replay in my head from time to time. At the age of 14, I had experienced a heartbreak that would leave a lifelong stain on my heart.

The type of period cramps I had every month was beyond excruciating. They left me always yearning for my mother's touch. Whenever she wasn't home, I would lie in her bed, waiting for her to get there. This day, in particular, my menstrual cramps were kicking my ass. My cycle was heavier than normal, so I figured I'd used two pads instead of one. My cousin was home with me this day, and I told her I was going to lay down in my mom's room until she got home. Before I laid down, I took my naproxen sodium that my doctor prescribed me for my cramps. I believe I slept for a little less than two hours when I heard the front door shut. I was in and out of sleep, so I dozed back off. I'm not sure how much time had passed before I felt a tight squeeze to my left hand. It was noticeable because my middle finger was in a splint after spraining it during a basketball game. I then felt someone breathing on my body's left side as I felt them rubbing up against my inner thigh. I went numb. I didn't know what to do at the moment, so I squeezed my eyes shut even tighter and remained frozen. As the hand got closer to my vagina area, I started to squirm in discomfort. The only thing that kept his hand from going any further was the texture of my pad that he could feel through my pajamas. He continued to rub until he just got up. I waited a few minutes before I opened my eyes. I was afraid of what I might see. When I was sure that the coast was clear, I jumped up and ran into my room and laid on the bottom bunk, and cried on my pillow. This man had just touched me in a way that was inappropriate for a girl my age. I didn't understand why a man who was old enough to be my father would even feel comfortable touching a child in that way. I questioned myself for the first few minutes. Why would I just lay there? Did he want to touch me for a while? Should I tell anyone? And then I ran out of my room and down the steps, looking for my house phone, as the tears

continued to fall. My cousin was thrown off because she could see

that I was in a rage. She asked several times, "What's wrong, Puff?

What's wrong? Why are you crying? Are you ok?" I couldn't utter

much besides, "I need to call my brother." It was at that moment I

knew he would protect me.

I found my phone and darted back up the steps. I

slammed my door and dialed his cell phone number. When he

answered, all he could hear was the agony in my voice from the

other side of the phone. "Puff, what's wrong?" he said. I was crying

hysterically when I uttered, "Where you at?" He said, "Calm down.

I went to pick my daughter up in Randallstown. What's wrong?" I

couldn't get it out. It was like a ball was stuck in my throat, and I

was trying to force the words out, "I need you to come home." He

replied, "What's wrong? What happened?" After seconds of silence

on the phone, I finally could speak. "He was touching on me. He

only stopped because he felt my pad." The anger resonated from

his voice, "What? Man, I'm on my way." I heard an instant knock

on the door. A voice followed, "Can we call your mother?" I

ignored him. I was angry. I wanted to hurt him. He asked again. This time he was saying, "Can we please just call your mother." I couldn't bear speaking to him. I continued looking out my window at the front lawn, waiting for my brother to pull up. Time seemed to have flown because he got there quicker than I could've imagined. As he began to get out of the car, I heard the back door shut. I ran to the bathroom, located in the back of the house, to see this man running down the alley with a market bag. My brother entered the house, and I ran down the steps. He placed my niece's car seat on the living room floor and asked me, "Where that nigga at?" I responded, "He ran up the alley." My brother flew out the back door. Hours had passed, and my brother still hadn't returned. I didn't have a clue what had taken place until that evening when I was being interrogated. The first question, "What happened?" I didn't feel comfortable speaking, so I just stared off into a daze. They asked me again with more bass, this time. I replied frantically, "He was touching on me. He was feeling on my body through my pants." The tears started to pour. I was embarrassed. The next question, "Why did you call your brother instead of calling your mother?" In my head, I was thinking, what the hell is she going to do. She's a woman, and he's a man. I wanted him to get his ass beat. I wanted him to feel how I felt. So, I didn't respond. Then came the words that would haunt me for the rest of my life. "You know if that man presses charges on your brother, you could go to jail too, right? Your brother busted that man head open with a bat and left him in the alley to die." All I could do was ask myself, was I the victim or the suspect? How the hell was they more concerned about his ass than mine?

Although I didn't want him to die, he deserved it. I yelled out, "He knew he was guilty. That's why he ran. He left with a bag. Why are ya'll fussing at me?" Before I knew it, a phone call was being made on speaker. It was the head of our family's voice coming through the phone. The conversation was one-sided as they updated him on what had happened that day. The way they were putting it was as if his injury was more important than him violating me. "Where is she?" was the next thing, he said. I picked up the phone and said, "Hello." His words would cut me deep as if I wasn't already trying to erase the comment from an hour before. "You listen to me. I'm going to visit that man in the hospital. I'm going to look him in the eyes, and if he doesn't show any signs of guilt, I'm going to whip your ass." I really couldn't believe what I had just heard from my granddad. It was like someone stabbed me with a knife and continued to twist it until they were ready to rip my heart out. How could the people who were supposed to protect me make me feel abandoned? Just when I thought it couldn't get any worst, the next day, it did. I was forced to see this man while he laid in a hospital bed for his pedophilia actions.

We left the hospital after hours of anticipation, me not knowing what my fate would be. The beating never happened. No apologies were given from anyone. Days had gone by, and it was like time was standing still in my life. Things went back to normal for everyone else involved except me. I was creating hate in my heart for any man standing who had balls between their legs. I never wanted to be left alone with a man again in fear that they would try to do something to me. I went through high school with a vengeance. I made every guy pay for what had happened to me.

I would purposely make them fall in love with me knowing I was just going to dump their asses. A few of them thought they were going to play me, but I was ten steps ahead.

I remember dating this one guy after I had already smashed his best friend. I didn't like his best friend, but I used him as bait to get back at his girlfriend, who cheated on him with my friend's boyfriend. They thought they were running games when I was only dating him to cover up the fact that I had a girlfriend. I had a love for women since the age of seven, but I still hadn't come out to the world yet. He didn't know it, but I had already lost my virginity two years before to my ex-girlfriend. Our short-lived relationship came to an end when I got tired of his shit. I had it set in my mind that I wasn't going to walk away quietly. I was going to go out with a bang. I laughed at the end of our last argument while saying, "You just mad because I'm leaving your dumb ass for a girl." Well, he wasn't going to go out like a sucker, so he grabbed my ass, and we tussled to the floor. I left that night with carpet burns. I still wanted the last laugh, so when I saw him and his best friend the following week, I started talking more shit. I had found myself losing again as they put me in the back of his best friend's trunk and took me for a spin. I took another L. I got the picture and went on with my life, looking for my next victim.

I was inflicting my hurt on to one guy after the next. They were my secret lovers while I praised my relationships with women in public. At the age of 25, my karma had finally started catching up to me. I ended up being in a relationship with someone who would later inflict their childhood scars on my life. It ended with her going to jail for domestic violence. It was then that I knew I needed counseling to heal my scars from my childhood. I finally had enough. I knew I had to find a way to move past the hurt. When I met my therapist, she could tell I was broken just by our first conversation. She didn't know what had happened yet, but she knew I had experienced some type of tragedy and that I was looking for answers and apologies that I had never gotten. I was doing too much, blaming others and not taking any accountability for my actions. I never wanted to admit it, but I had deep-rooted trust issues. I felt like anyone who showed interest in me only wanted something from me. If people I thought truly loved me could hurt me, why wouldn't anyone else?

As the sessions went on, she told me that she had realized a pattern. I was the queen of the cat and mouse game. I only wanted people who didn't want me at first. I would continue to chase them for the thrill. Once I figured out a way for them to become head over heels, I'd leave. I didn't know how to accept people being good to me. She finally got the truth out of me when she asked me to go back to my childhood and tell her about a trauma. She told me when I could give her the real answer; then we could start there. I could start righting my wrongs. I told her what happened and that even ten years later, no one ever apologized. I had never received the closure I thought I deserved. I never realized that holding onto the what-ifs had kept me captive. She went on to tell me the harsh truth. "You're waiting on an apology that you probably will never get. If they haven't apologized thus far, they probably never will. And that's ok. You have to forgive them for you. As long as you don't, your world will never spin for you. You're still trapped in your fourteen-year-old body, and you have to heal her." It made sense all of a sudden, and the tears started to pour.

For the next few sessions, forgiveness was the topic of discussion. She helped me release his demons from my inner soul. I started changing immediately. I wanted to teach people the importance of forgiveness. I wanted to support more women because you never know how much pain they hide behind their smiles. I created my brand, "I Wasn't Built To Break!!" and never looked back.

For years I was looking for an explanation of why I wasn't important enough to receive an apology that I felt I deserved. But why did I expect someone to say sorry if they didn't feel that way in their heart? Even if they were, they could never face me without sulking in their guilt. Either way, I knew I had to find it in my heart to let God have the final say. I came to terms with my inability to apologize when I was wrong because I thought that was the norm. I never learned how important it was to offer an apology. I started by apologizing to myself for all the years I held on to hurt. For all the hearts I broke because I was too weak to heal myself. I've made plenty of mistakes in life due to that situation. Yet, I've also used that pain to grow. Three and a half years later, here I am. I am still working on my heart and the art of forgiveness. I encourage each person to understand the importance of forgiveness.

1. It's for YOU!

2. Half the time, we want an apology to justify a person's action to give them another chance.

3. Just because we can use glue to fix things doesn't mean it won't break again.

4. You can forgive someone and still love them from a distance.

5. If you don't forgive for yourself, the person/thing will have power over you for years to come.

6. Repeated behavior shows there was no real truth behind the apology.

7. You are not free until you aren't mad anymore.

8. You have to also forgive yourself.

9. You MUST heal what hurt you. You owe it to yourself not to waste years holding on to hurt.

10. They say you have 24 hours to cry about your pain. I say take as

    much time as you need. No one knows how your pain affects you.

Learning Your Love Language

Would you rather have someone tell you how much you mean to them by putting their feelings inside of a card and giving it to you or giving you a $200 gift card? I would rather have the card. The gift card has no meaning behind it.

We all want somebody to love us the way we want to be loved. Yet, half of us don't even know how we want to be loved. When a person asks what do you want from me, the most common response is, I want loyalty, trust, and for you to communicate. We always give answers associated with characteristics. It's rarely ever made clear what gestures we expect.

Gary Chapman, the man behind the five-love language test, came up with a way to help couples better understand each other. Millions of people across the world have used this test to enhance their bonds with their significant others. Back in 2016, my marriage had begun taking a turn for the worst. My ex-wife and I decided to go to therapy, hoping to save our marriage. Our therapist recommended that both of us take the test to better understand ourselves and the other. The test is set up with various questions asking what gesture out of two different situations would be more important. When the test is over, your love language is broken down into a percentage in each of the five categories. The five categories are words of affirmation, acts of service, receiving gifts, quality time, and physical touch. Before I took the test, all I knew in my mind was that I wanted someone who equally loved me back. Someone who wouldn't cheat on me. A person who loved me out loud and not in private. I thought having a person's trust, and loyalty was all a relationship took. If my person was willing to communicate and express their feelings, I was good to go.

After we took the test, I understood why we didn't get along often. I was loving her in ways that I thought were the right way. She was doing the same. At the time, my love language was acts of service. I was a stay-at-home wife, but I was a full-time student taking seven classes while being a full-time mom. I always appreciated the extra help. She worked from 5 am to 7 pm most days, so she barely ever had time to assist me around the house.

For her, she enjoyed the physical touch. I was so busy with school that I barely ever made time to give her any physical attention. When she would want sex, I just wasn't in the mood. When I'm in grind mode or school mode, it tends to be the only thing my mind can focus on. It wasn't on purpose; that's just how I had always been. The test worked for a good while, and our marriage started doing a complete turnaround. I decided then to purchase the book to get an even better understanding of myself and why I yearned for certain things. It has now become a way of life for me.

I introduced this test to all of my friends and potential love interests when I think we will make it to the next level. Personally, I think that this test should be taken at least once a year because our wants and desires tend to change. Years ago, I couldn't stand being up under my partner a lot because I felt like I needed time to miss them. Now, in this current time, my love language is quality time. I no longer get a thrill out of hanging outside with my girlfriends. I would rather be laid up watching movies, eating cookies and ice cream with my lover.

86

I look forward to coming home to someone and preparing hot meals for them. I no longer have the luxury of wasting time because I have two young men who I take pride in raising, and they need stability. If you want your relationship to work, I suggest you take the test even if you don't purchase the book.

Bonus: Learning to Accept Love

As I continue my journey to self-love, I know that it is important for me to learn how to accept love. After constant heartbreak, I had conditioned myself to push away anyone who tried to get close to me. I decided to take a break from love. Ever since I was 17, I've been in ongoing relationships. I never really had time to process my situations and fully heal. I just felt like love wasn't for me.

In July of 2020, I met a guy randomly through a mutual party. He and I truly never had any intentions of dating. At the time, I was in a complicated relationship with my youngest son's father. We communicated every so often in the beginning. He knew what my situation was from the jump, and honestly, he respected it. One evening he and I were texting about how I whipped his ass in Uno when we first met. I'm a very competitive person when it comes to board/card games. He challenged me for a rematch, so I had decided to invite him over. Normally, I would refrain from any new guys meeting my children, but he had already been around my newborn a couple of times when we were

at his brother's house.

We became really good friends. He started helping me

with various things due to the lack of assistance I was getting. He

did market runs with and for me. He came over and just took out

the trash. He even got me out the house and took me out for food

and drinks. He was such a genuine guy. He did so many things for

me without me having to ask. I had never experienced anything

like it before. Most men who had been in my presence for months

would've at least tried to press up on me to get between my legs.

That wasn't his plan, though. When I felt stressed, he offered to

walk with me around the water to put my mind at ease. He was

showing me a different side of men that I had never experienced

in my adult years. Yet, with all that, I still refused to allow myself

to get attached. In my mind, I believed he would be just like the

rest.

As time went on, none of his ways changed. He remained

the same gentleman I had met four months prior. The things I had

prayed for were coming to life. I would tell my friends that I had finally found my "Russell." Even though I felt this way, I went out of my way to never let him see me weak. Out of all the things that I had admired about him, how he interacted with my children was what I loved the most. He was truly trying to invest in me. Whenever we talked about life, he would always bring up my goals. Some of them that he heard me speaking about from paying attention from the sideline. He was a critical thinker and put thought into a lot of things that we spoke about. The fact that a man was so in tune with me, setting goals and accomplishing them was astonishing.

I told him when we first met that I had started writing a book about my life. Since I was going through postpartum depression, I had put that on hold. I have yet to get back to it because I began focusing on writing this guide to self-love. He hasn't forgotten about it and still brings it up to make sure that I have intentions of finishing that book. Since we've met, he's been my biggest cheerleader. I took a gun license class in August, but due to me being guilty of 21 assault charges at the age of fifteen, they denied me. I got very discouraged. I didn't even care that I was about to let the money I paid for the class go down the drain. Not him. He encouraged me to file an appeal and offered to buy me my first gun once the process was finished. As of right now, my expungement is in the process of being deleted. I truly can't thank that man enough. He had my back even when he didn't have to. Things haven't been all sweet between us due to my insecurities. However, I truly wouldn't trade the friend in him for anything in this world.

This man is the reason why I need to get back to the woman who values herself. Being loved correctly has shown me that I don't have to settle. I don't have to tolerate being half-loved by a man who brings nothing to the table but potential. I'm learning to trust my feelings and not let my past interfere with something good. I know that I'm growing in love because I have never trusted anyone with my finances. I never wanted to learn how to be gentle with a man. To speak and not to yell when we're disagreeing. To respect his mind when he makes certain decisions. I'm learning that it's the man's job to lead and my job to follow. This man truly has made everything seem so easy. He's the true definition of a man who's willing to give up the I's for the US. Although I know that I am a work in progress, this man has shown me what it is to feel valued and loved effortlessly.

29 Reasons Vs. 29 Questions

On April 12, 2021, I turned 29 years old. This year is special to me for many reasons. First, I am grateful that God has allowed me to travel around the sun 29 times. Second, this is my last year in my twenties. Some would like to think of it as my last year of fucks up. I look at it as the year that I set goals and accomplish them. I have also made it clear to myself that I refuse to go backward in some areas of my life. I don't expect to be perfect, but I now know what I have to do to be the person I want to be. In honor of my 29th birthday, I figured I could give you 29 reasons why I wrote this guide to self-love. I will then give you 29 questions to ask yourself.

93

My 29 Reasons

1. I want every woman to know she's NOT ALONE!
2. I struggled with being a single mother.
3. I talked to my friends before I talked to GOD.
4. I am my worst critic.
5. I suffer from anxiety and depression.
6. I cry often.
7. I didn't know my worth.
8. I loved for the wrong reasons.
9. I built relationships/friendships through trauma bonding.
10. My three older brothers were incarcerated in front of the world.
11. I've been heartbroken.
12. I've been used.
13. I allowed my son's father to control me.
14. I struggle with choosing ME!
15. I stayed in toxic relationships too long.
16. My friends abandoned me.
17. I abandoned myself.
18. I suck at forgiveness.
19. My parents hurt me.
20. I went from being the ONLY one to a side bitch.
21. I allowed social media to cloud my judgment.
22. I am a catastrophic thinker.
23. I lost myself loving someone else.
24. I said yes when I wanted to say no.
25. I needed an outlet.
26. I am NOT perfect.
27. I screamed when I should have spoken.
28. My marriage failed because we failed each other.
29. I had to forgive motherfuckers who weren't even sorry.

My 29 Questions

1. Have you ever told yourself that you love yourself?

   _____

   _____

   _____

   _____

2. Have you ever stayed in a relationship because of the time invested even though you knew in your heart it was already over?

   _____

   _____

   _____

   _____

3. Have you ever been cheated on?

   _____

   _____

   _____

   _____

4. Do you know the worst thing you dislike about yourself?

   _____

   _____

   _____

   _____

5. Do you know what your worth is?

_____

_____

_____

_____

6. What's your greatest strength?

_____

_____

_____

_____

7. What's your biggest flaw?

_____

_____

_____

_____

8. What's your biggest fear?

_____

_____

_____

_____

9. When was the last time you cried?

_____

_____

_____

_____

10. What makes you angry?

_____

_____

_____

_____

11. What's your greatest weakness?

_____

_____

_____

_____

12. Have you ever been in love?

_____

_____

_____

_____

13. Have you ever been betrayed by any of your friends?

_____

_____

_____

_____

14. Do you believe in abortions?

_____

_____

_____

_____

15. What's the first physical feature you look at on strangers?

16. What's a characteristic that your partner must have?

17. Do you feel the need to still speak with any of your exes?

18. Are you in a relationship because you are content or happy?

19. Has your pride caused you to lose out on a relationship or friendship?

20. Do you have any regrets?

_____

_____

_____

_____

21. Do you truly trust your best friend?

_____

_____

_____

_____

22. Have you ever taken yourself out on a date?

_____

_____

_____

_____

23. What's the worst thing you've ever said about someone?

_____

_____

_____

_____

24. Have you struggled with confidence or self-doubt?

_____

_____

_____

_____

25. Which one of your bad habits is the hardest to break?

_____

_____

_____

_____

26. Would you rather be hurt by the person you love the most or trust the most?

_____

_____

_____

_____

27. Is bad sex a deal-breaker?

_____

_____

_____

_____

28. How do you handle stress?

_____

_____

_____

_____

29. Are you truly happy?

_____

_____

_____

_____

I ask these 29 questions so that, for once, we can be honest with ourselves. Some of us refuse to accept our lives for exactly what they are. Although I didn't ask you publicly, I encourage you to answer these questions honestly. Just remember, to move forward in life, you have to be honest about who you are and the things you want. While some of these questions are easy to answer, others require you to dig deep. DO IT!! I'm cheering you on from the sidelines. From this day forward, I'm encouraging you to be the BEST version of yourself!

Acknowledgments

To the most high, thank you for always keeping me...keeping your hands wrapped around me in times where I thought giving up was the answer. Thank you for blessing me with two boys that give me a reason to always strive for greatness. Now that I'm putting you first, my life has been changing for the better. I am now learning that when something happens unexpectedly, you're testing my growth. Through you, I have learned to find the blessing in all things. Because of you, I have strength.

To my supporters, thank you. For always encouraging me to keep going. For never judging me for my past, but instead giving praise for my testimony. For helping me accomplish a goal by setting a deadline for this book. Ya'll pushed me to the finish line. Forever grateful for that.

To my sisters, because all of you are more than just my friends, thanks. Thanks for always having my back. Listening to me cry. You all pull me up when I need a hand. Thank you for supporting me in everything that I do. Never judging me for staying in toxic situations longer than I should have. Thanks for always holding me accountable. Not many have people that will tell them what they NEED to hear vs. what they want to hear. I love you, girls. I am blessed to have bonus sisters.

To my mother. There are not enough words to describe the thanks I want to give to you. I could never thank you enough. Although we've had a rocky relationship throughout my teenage/adult years, you still are my everything. I never understood why you were so hard on me as a child. As a result, I am a WOMAN with morals. You believed in me before I knew how to believe in myself. Thank you for understanding me individually from the rest of your children. You are the reason I am strong. I appreciate all that you continue to do for my sons and me. Thanks for having my back whenever times get hard for me. I understand you more now than I ever have. You have a heart of gold. Don't ever let anyone tell you that you are not worthy. I Love you beyond life!

To my siblings, thanks for always being willing to go to war for me. Ya'll have given me memories that will last me a lifetime. Because of ya'll, my children get to grow up with a ton of cousins. I promise to always look out for y'all children as if they were mine.

To my dear friend Star, you hold a very special place in my heart. You are the true definition of ride or die. From the beginning of our friendship until now, I have never questioned your loyalty to me. You've shown me how to be fearless. I admire your ability to simply just be you. You aren't afraid to show the world exactly who you are. You've never asked me for anything that you weren't willing to give in return. You share your opinions with me without making me feel judged. When I think of someone who stays 100% true to self, it's you. Your courage to always stand in your truth is something I will always commend you for.

To my bonus brother, Kamau, I appreciate you so much. I can always count on you to help me see my vision through. Each time I've come to you for your assistance, you have never steered me wrong. Whether it's just simple advice or helping me choose a book cover. Together, you and I have created greatness. People tell me all the time how much our podcast has helped them in certain areas of their lives. Thanks for being my brother and never trying your hand when I was vulnerable. So grateful God placed you in my life. You have a sister in me for life.

To the man who came into my life looking for nothing in return, thank you for loving me when I wasn't capable of loving myself. You seen the light in me even when I was in a dark place. I know that I haven't been the easiest to deal with, but I'm grateful that you haven't given up on me.

A Letter To My Young Kings

There's nothing in this world that I could ever be more grateful for. Bralyn, my life started when I had you. D'Artagnan Jr., life transformed when I had you. Together, the both of you make me who I am. As I always say, Bralyn, you taught me to be humble. DJ, you taught me patience. I will always work my hardest to be the best role model to both of you. Life gets hard, but as long as I have you two, I know I have a purpose. I refuse to allow you kings to ever to see me fold. I don't have it altogether, and at times I feel like I've failed, but I don't lose. I learn. They say the greatest creation is to bear a child. I was blessed to bear two. I will always encourage you both to go for whatever dreams you have, no matter if they are big or small. I'll teach you both that it's okay for men to cry. Show your emotions. It shows your strength. Always respect women as you'd like a man to respect your mother. Always take the high road. You will never have to fight battles alone. Momma will always be there. I'll be ya'll strength when the going gets tough. I Love You, boys, with every ounce of my body. Thanks for sticking it out with me thus far. Thanks for always giving me a

reason to keep at it. No matter how old you boys get, Bralyn, you'll

forever be my Mooch and DJ; you'll always be my Bookie Bookie

(Shinky Butt). To the two young men who've heard my heartbeat

on the inside, I Love You For Life & After.

Momma Bear

for sticking it out with me thus far. Thanks for always giving me a reason to keep at it. No matter how old you boys get, Bralyn, you'll forever be my Mooch and DJ; you'll always be my Bookie Bookie (Shinky Butt). To the two young men who've heard my heartbeat on the inside, I Love You For Life & After.

Momma Bear

CPSIA information can be obtained
at www.ICGtesting.com
Printed in the USA
BVHW071933100621
609270BV00004B/476